SARAH BRO

# VEGETAR

cooking

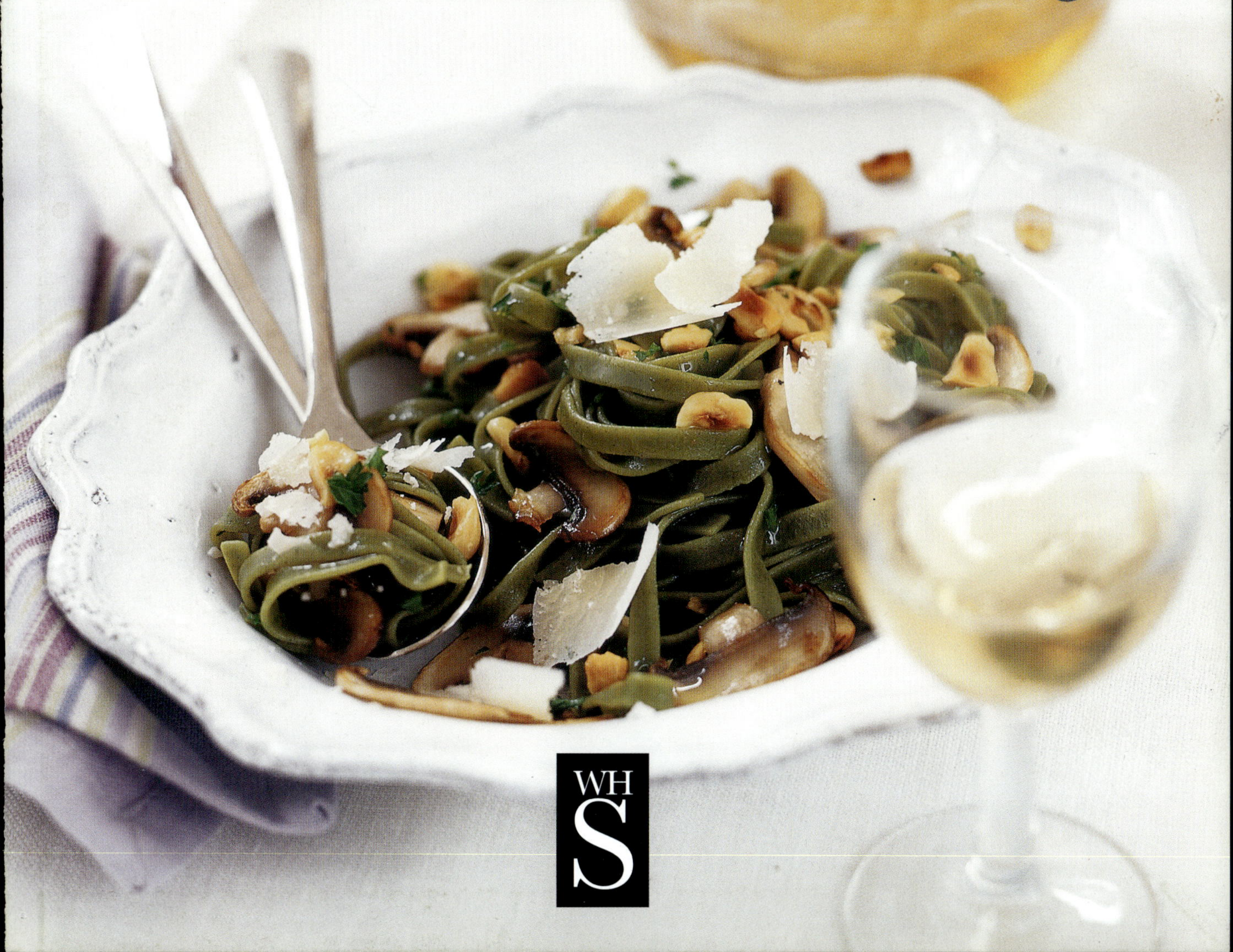

WH S

This edition first published in Great Britain in 2002 by Ebury Press
for WHSmith, Greenbridge Road, Swindon SN3 3LD

1 3 5 7 9 10 8 6 4 2



Ebury Press
Random House, 20 Vauxhall Bridge Road, London SW1V 2SA

Random House Australia (Pty) Limited|
20 Alfred Street, Milsons Point, Sydney, New South Wales 2061, Australia

Random House New Zealand Limited
18 Poland Road, Glenfield, Auckland 10, New Zealand

Random House South Africa (Pty) Limited
Endulini, 5A Jubilee Road, Parktown 2193, South Africa

The Random House Group Limited Reg. No. 954009
www.randomhouse.co.uk

A CIP catalogue record for this book is available from the British Library.

Editor: Gillian Haslam
Designer: Christine Wood
Photographer: Jean Cazals and Craig Robertson
Food Stylist: Marie-Ange Lapierre and Jules Beresford
Stylist: Roísín Nield and Helen Trent

ISBN 0091884063

Papers used by Ebury Press are natural, recyclable products made from wood grown in sustainable forests.

Printed and bound in Italy by Graphicom srl.

# CONTENTS



*Title page: Spinach Tagliatelle with Button Mushrooms and Hazelnuts, page 44*

*Above: Spiced Tofu and Vegetable Tagine, page 68*

# INTRODUCTION

Many people want to eat less meat these days for all sorts of reasons – health, food scares, allergies or concern for animal welfare. But what no one wants is to spend hours shopping or ages in the kitchen. I've written this book for all those who, like me, want to eat good vegetarian food but don't want to feel that it will take an enormous amount of effort.

When I first started writing vegetarian recipes, my main concern was to reassure people that they could have a highly nutritious diet without eating meat or fish. I also wanted to blur the distinction between meat meals and meat-free meals, so that vegetarian fare could be seen as entirely acceptable mainstream food. Whilst many people now readily eat meat-free meals, one of the remaining myths of vegetarian cookery is that cooking without meat is somehow more trouble. I hope this book will dispel that myth.

I have always written from personal experience. Like many others, I am juggling both a career and parenthood as well as wanting time for numerous other interests. My recipes are by necessity simple and speedy. True, I have now had over twenty years of experience cooking this sort of food, but many changes in the last decade or so have made getting and preparing good food easier. For example, most large supermarkets stock an excellent range of vegetarian basics plus a huge selection of fruit and vegetables. Even specialist ingredients are no longer hard to find.

Throughout the book you'll find extra tips on cooking techniques, and what to look for when buying and storing less familiar ingredients. I hope the recipes that follow will help you discover how easy and simple vegetarian food can be to prepare. After all, if it has been no fuss to assemble, you'll find it even more enjoyable to eat.

Sarah Brown

*Ten-Minute Standby Supper, page 42*

# SOUPS, starters and snacks

# SPICED DHAL SOUP

SERVES: 4 PREPARATION: 15 MINS COOKING: 1 HOUR

INGREDIENTS

2 tbsp sunflower oil
2 carrots, peeled and diced
1 large potato, peeled and diced
100 g (4 oz) frozen peas
1 onion, peeled and chopped
¼ tsp chilli powder
½ tsp turmeric
½ tsp mustard powder
400 g (14 oz) tin chopped tomatoes
1 tbsp tomato purée
50 g (2 oz) red lentils
1 cm (½ in) piece of root ginger, peeled and grated
3 cloves
juice of ½ lemon
1 tsp sugar
about 600 ml (1 pint) vegetable stock
salt
2–3 tbsp chopped fresh coriander

NUTRITION

*Each portion contains:*

*Energy: 182 calories*

*Fat: 6 g of which saturates 0.8 g*

1 In a large saucepan, heat the oil and gently fry the carrots, potato, peas and onion. Sprinkle over the chilli powder, turmeric and mustard and stir well. Cook the vegetables until fairly soft, stirring frequently.

2 Add the chopped tomatoes, tomato purée, red lentils, ginger, cloves, lemon juice and sugar. Pour in the stock. Bring to the boil, then simmer for about 1 hour or until the lentils are very soft. Stir occasionally during cooking and add more stock if necessary. Season with salt.

3 Just before serving, stir in most of the fresh coriander; use the rest to garnish each bowl.

COOK'S TIP

This soup, with its colourful mixture of vegetables and lentils cooked in a spiced tomato stock, is almost a meal in itself and is good served with naan bread. Alternatively, go for a salad. This soup will freeze, but do not keep it very long because the spices will lose their flavour. If you find a recipe a bit too spicy, adding extra sugar and salt can help reduce the temperature.

# BUTTERNUT AND CARROT SOUP WITH GINGER

SERVES: 4 PREPARATION: 15 MINS COOKING: 50 MINS

## INGREDIENTS

2 tbsp sunflower oil
1 onion, peeled and chopped
1 clove garlic, peeled and crushed
1 tsp freshly grated root ginger
700 g (1½ lb) butternut squash, seeds and fibres removed (not peeled), then chopped
250 g (8 oz) carrots, peeled and chopped
600–900 ml (1–1½ pints) vegetable stock
2 tsp fresh thyme
1 bay leaf
grated zest and juice of 1 lemon
salt and pepper

## NUTRITION

*Each portion contains:*
*Energy: 150 calories*
*Fat: 6 g of which saturates 0.7 g*

1 In a large saucepan, heat the oil and gently cook the onion and garlic. Add the ginger, butternut squash and carrots and cook gently, covered, for 10 minutes.

2 Add the stock, thyme and bay leaf. Bring to the boil, then cover the pan again and simmer for 40 minutes or until the vegetables are really tender.

3 Cool slightly, then remove the bay leaf and whizz the soup in a blender or food processor until smooth. Season to taste with lemon zest and juice, salt and pepper. Reheat before serving. For a special occasion, garnish each serving with a swirl of cream or soured cream.

### COOK'S TIP

With its warm orange colour and delicate nutty flavour, butternut squash is a versatile vegetable, useful in casseroles, roasted vegetable combinations and, especially, soup. It has similarities with root vegetables such as carrots and parsnips in that, once cooked, it will purée to a smooth, creamy consistency. I've added some carrots to enhance the colour, and ginger for a warm flavour. Although the outer skin looks indigestible, it becomes tender during cooking and will purée to a smooth texture. By not peeling the squash you'll save time and this will also increase the flavour of the finished soup.

# DEEP GREEN WATERCRESS SOUP

SERVES: 4 PREPARATION: 10 MINS COOKING: 30 MINS

## INGREDIENTS

2 tbsp olive oil
1 onion, peeled and finely chopped
1 small potato, peeled and chopped
2 or 3 packets of watercress, washed
600 ml (1 pint) vegetable stock
salt and pepper

## NUTRITION

*Each portion contains:*

*Energy: 95 calories*

*Fat: 6 g of which saturates 1 g*

1 Heat the oil in a saucepan and cook the onion gently for about 5 minutes. Add the potato and watercress and 'sweat' the vegetables, covered, for about 3 minutes. Pour on the stock and bring to the boil. Cover the pan again and simmer for about 20 minutes or until the potatoes are very soft.

2 Allow the soup to cool for a few minutes, then whizz in a food processor or blender until smooth. Season to taste.

3 Return the soup to the pan and heat through before serving.

### COOK'S TIP

This is a marvellous soup, with good colour and a smooth texture, and it's packed full of vitamins. I often make it in the colder months as it seems to give me a real boost as well as warding off winter chills. Serve it as a light snack on its own, or as a starter before a more substantial dish. For a richer version, stir in some crème fraîche just before serving.

# RED PEPPER, TOMATO AND TOFU SOUP

SERVES: 4 PREPARATION: 15 MINS COOKING: 1 HOUR

## INGREDIENTS

2 medium-sized red peppers
2 tbsp olive oil
1 onion, peeled and finely chopped
1 clove garlic, peeled and crushed
1 tsp dried oregano or marjoram
1 tsp dried thyme
400 g (14 oz) tin chopped tomatoes
2 tbsp tomato purée
300 ml (½ pint) vegetable stock
285 g (9 oz) tofu
salt and pepper

## NUTRITION

*Each portion contains:*

*Energy: 160 calories*

*Fat: 9 g of which saturates 1 g*

1 Preheat the oven to 200°C/400°F/gas 6. Lightly oil the peppers and pierce once or twice. Roast in the oven for 30 minutes or until well charred on all sides. Cool, then peel off the skin and remove the seeds. Chop the flesh roughly.

2 In a large saucepan, heat the rest of the oil and gently fry the onion and garlic until soft. Add the chopped red peppers, herbs, tinned tomatoes, tomato purée and stock. Bring the mixture to the boil, then cover and simmer for 30 minutes. Leave to cool slightly.

3 Whizz the tofu in a blender or food processor with 150ml (¼ pint) water or stock until completely smooth. Add the tomato and pepper mixture and whizz until smooth. Season well, and heat through gently before serving.

### COOK'S TIP

Tofu is made from processed soya beans and has a firm texture which makes it suitable for slicing and cubing. When making soup, the tofu needs to be blended with water until creamy so the final result will be smooth. A blender is best. You can use a food processor but the soup may be slightly grainy.

*See full picture on page 16.*

# CORN BREAD

SERVES: 4 PREPARATION: 15 MINS COOKING: 20 MINS

## INGREDIENTS

125 g (4 oz) wholemeal flour
125 g (4 oz) maize flour (corn meal)
1 tbsp caster sugar
2 tsp baking powder
½ tsp salt
1 tsp toasted cumin seeds
2 eggs
250 ml (8 fl oz) milk
2 tbsp sunflower oil

## NUTRITION

*Each portion contains:*

*Energy: 360 calories*

*Fat: 13 g of which saturates 3 g*

1 Preheat the oven to 200°C/400°F/gas 6. Combine the wholemeal flour, maize flour, sugar, baking powder, salt and toasted cumin seeds in a large bowl.

2 In a jug, beat the eggs with the milk, then add the oil. Add this liquid to the dry ingredients and mix quickly.

3 Pour the mixture into a greased tin measuring 20 x 20 cm (8 x 8 in). Bake in the oven for 20 minutes. Serve the corn bread cut in squares, either hot or warm.

### COOK'S TIP

Made from golden maize flour, this bread is very easy – just a quick mixing of wet and dry ingredients before baking. This version is made with milk and eggs which gives it a rich, slightly cake-like finish. It goes well with most casseroles and soups but especially those made with warming spices or sweet-flavoured vegetables. Best made and eaten on the same day.

*See full picture on page 16.*

# BRUSCHETTA

SERVES: 4 PREPARATION: 15 MINS COOKING: 5–7 MINS

## INGREDIENTS

1 ciabatta loaf, cut in slices
1–2 cloves garlic, peeled and halved
olive oil
freshly grated Parmesan cheese

For the roast red pepper and olive topping:
2 red peppers
125 g (4 oz) pitted black olives, chopped
2 tbsp sun-dried tomato paste
2 tsp capers
2 tsp chopped fresh oregano
salt and pepper

For the onion, caper and feta cheese topping:
2–3 tbsp olive oil
2–3 medium onions, peeled and cut into thin rings
salt and pepper
2 tbsp capers
50–75 g (2–3 oz) feta cheese, crumbled

1 Preheat the oven to 200°C/400°F/gas 6. Bake the slices of bread for 5–7 minutes. Rub the surfaces with garlic and then brush with olive oil. Sprinkle with a little cheese and bake again briefly.

2 Roast Red Pepper and Olive topping : Roast and peel the peppers (see step 1, page 14). Chop the flesh finely and mix with the chopped olives, sun-dried tomato paste, capers and oregano. Season to taste with salt and pepper. Bake the bread as above, rub with garlic and brush with oil. Smear a little of the red pepper paste on each slice, then sprinkle on a little Parmesan. Serve immediately.

3 Onion, Caper and Feta Cheese topping: Make up the onion topping on page 58 (step 4) and keep it warm. Bake the bread as above, rub with garlic and brush with oil. Top with the warm onion mixture and sprinkle over the capers and feta cheese. Serve immediately.

## NUTRITION

*Each portion contains:*
*Without topping:*
*Energy: 190 calories*
*Fat: 10 g of which saturates 3 g*

*Roast red pepper and olive topping:*
*Energy: 250 calories*
*Fat: 14 g of which saturates 4 g*

*Onion, caper and feta cheese topping:*
*Energy: 246 calories*
*Fat: 9 g of which saturates 3 g*

### COOK'S TIP

Bruschetta are toasted slices of ciabatta or focaccia bread topped with a variety of flavourings. They make very simple snacks and great nibbles prior to a party meal. You can vary the toppings to fit in with whatever else you are serving.

# CASHEW AND MANGO SALAD WITH CITRUS DRESSING

SERVES: 4 PREPARATION: 15 MINS COOKING: 6 MINS

## INGREDIENTS

50 g (2 oz) cashew nuts
1 tbsp sesame seeds
1 large orange
50 ml (2 fl oz) sunflower oil
salt and pepper
1 mango
1 Romaine or Cos lettuce

## NUTRITION

*Each portion contains:*
*Energy: 220 calories*
*Fat: 18 g of which saturates 3 g*

1 Preheat the oven to 200°C/400°F/gas 6. Roast the cashew nuts in the oven for 5 minutes or until golden brown. Leave to cool, then chop very roughly. Toast the sesame seeds in a dry frying pan for 1 minute.

2 Remove the zest from the orange and reserve. Cut the fruit in half. Squeeze the juice from one half and mix with the oil. Add the orange zest. Season lightly. Peel and segment the remaining half. Put the segments in a bowl.

3 Peel the mango, cut round the stone and then cut the flesh into small pieces. Mix with the orange segments and add the toasted cashew nuts. Pour the orange juice and oil dressing over the fruit and nut mixture.

4 Line a bowl with lettuce leaves, pile in the fruit salad and garnish with the toasted sesame seeds. Serve immediately

## COOK'S TIP

This is a most refreshing savoury fruit salad. Serve it as a starter before a substantial main course, such as a pastry dish or casserole. It also works well as a side salad.

# OLIVE AND PEPPER STRUDELS

SERVES: 4 PREPARATION: 20 MINS COOKING: 50 MINS

### INGREDIENTS

For the filling:

1 red pepper

2 tbsp olive oil

1 onion, peeled and finely chopped

2 cloves garlic, peeled and crushed

8 sun-dried tomatoes (packed in oil)

125 g (4 oz) pitted black olives

4 tbsp chopped fresh basil

25 g (1 oz) pine kernels

salt and pepper

12 sheets of filo pastry

50–75 ml (2–3 fl oz) olive oil

### NUTRITION

*Each portion contains:*

*Energy: 370 calories*

*Fat: 28 g of which saturates 4 g*

1 Preheat the oven to 200°C/400°F/gas 6. Brush the red pepper with a little oil and pierce the skin. Roast in the oven for 30 minutes or until the skin is charred all over. Leave to cool, then peel off the skin and remove the seeds. Chop the flesh roughly. Leave the oven on, ready to cook the finished strudels.

2 Heat the rest of the oil in a saucepan and gently fry the onion and garlic until soft. Cool slightly, then scrape them with any oil into a food processor or blender. Add the red pepper, tomatoes, olives, basil and pine kernels. Process until fairly smooth. Season to taste. Divide into 12 portions.

3 Lay one sheet of filo pastry on the work surface and brush well with olive oil. Spoon a portion of filling in a line across the middle third of the sheet, leaving the side thirds clear and a small margin at the top. Fold over the margin to cover the filling, then fold in the sides. Roll up to make a cigar shape. Brush well with more oil and place on a baking tray. Repeat with the remaining sheets of pastry and filling.

4 Bake the strudels in the oven already preheated to 200°C/400°F/gas 6 for 20 minutes or until crisp. Serve warm or at room temperature.

### COOK'S TIP

Once the pepper is roasted, the filling is very easy to make using a food processor or blender. I think filo is best eaten on the day it is made, but at a pinch these would last to a second day if kept in the fridge.

# ASPARAGUS WITH LEMON AND ROASTED HAZELNUTS

SERVES: 4 PREPARATION: 15 MINS COOKING: 15 MINS

## INGREDIENTS

For the dressing:

75 g (3 oz) hazelnuts

2 tbsp mixed chopped fresh parsley and tarragon

2 tbsp lemon juice

1 clove garlic, peeled

salt and pepper

150 ml (¼ pint) mixed hazelnut oil and olive oil

1 tsp grated lemon zest

2 bunches of asparagus

## NUTRITION

*Each portion contains:*

*Energy: 380 calories*

*Fat: 39 g, of which saturates 5 g*

1 First, make the dressing. Preheat the oven to 190°C/375°F/gas 5. Toast the hazelnuts in the oven for 5-6 minutes. Cool, then rub off the skins using your hands or by rolling them in a cloth.

2 Roughly chop 25 g (1 oz) of the hazelnuts and set aside. Finely grind the remaining nuts in a blender or food processor.

3 Add the herbs and blend thoroughly for a few seconds. Add the lemon juice, garlic and seasoning. Blend again, then gradually add the oil with the machine running. Finally, stir in the lemon zest and adjust the seasoning.

4 Prepare the asparagus by trimming off the woody stem ends. Place upright in a tall saucepan of boiling water, with the stems in the water and the tips above so they steam. Cook for 8-10 minutes. Drain well and leave to cool.

5 Arrange each portion on individual plates and pour some of the dressing over. Garnish with the chopped roasted hazelnuts.

### COOK'S TIP

Asparagus makes an easy and elegant starter. For an even simpler version, just serve the asparagus with melted butter and garnish with roasted hazelnuts. When cooking the asparagus, tying the stems loosely together with string will help keep them upright in the saucepan. Half a lemon will yield 2 tbsp juice.

# BARBECUED HALOUMI CHEESE BAGUETTE

SERVES: 4 PREPARATION: 15 MINS COOKING: 15 MINS

## INGREDIENTS

450 g (1 lb) Haloumi cheese, sliced
selection of vegetables (mixed coloured peppers, aubergine, field mushrooms, tinned artichoke hearts)
olive oil
4 baguettes, split open
1–2 tbsp chopped fresh mint

## NUTRITION

*Each portion contains:*
*Energy: 640 calories*
*Fat: 41 g of which saturates 16 g*

1 Prepare the vegetables: quarter and de-seed the peppers, thickly slice the aubergine and field mushrooms and cut the artichoke hearts in half. Brush the vegetables with olive oil and barbecue over a charcoal fire until tender and lightly charred all over, turning regularly during the cooking. Set aside.

2 Barbecue the cheese slices until just heated through. The cheese slices can be put directly on the grill over the coals for about 30 seconds, but the cheese will drip as it melts. I prefer to put the slices on foil, then on the grill. They take longer to heat, but it is less messy.

3 Lightly toast the cut sides of the baguettes on the barbecue. Top with a mixture of vegetables and slices of cheese. Add a little chopped mint before handing round.

### COOK'S TIP

Haloumi is a semi-hard Cypriot cheese made from ewe's milk, and is available in most supermarkets. It is excellent for cooking on a grill as it develops in flavour when cooked but doesn't melt away to nothing.

# MAIN
## courses

# GOAT'S CHEESE AND ASPARAGUS SALAD

SERVES: 4 PREPARATION: 15 MINS COOKING: 15 MINS

INGREDIENTS

350 g (12 oz) asparagus
450 g (1 lb) small new potatoes
6 tbsp salsa verde (see Cook's Tip)
250 g (8 oz) goat's cheese
mixed salad leaves including some fresh basil leaves
1–2 tbsp freshly shaved Parmesan

NUTRITION

*Each portion contains:*
*Energy: 360 calories*
*Fat: 24 g of which saturates 10 g*

1 Trim the asparagus and steam for 8–10 minutes or until tender. Leave to cool.

2 Cook the new potatoes in boiling water until tender. Drain and mix with the salsa verde while still warm. Cut the cheese into 8 slices.

3 Arrange the asparagus, potatoes and cheese on a bed of mixed salad leaves. Garnish with Parmesan shavings and serve immediately with crust granary or sunflower-seed bread and butter.

**COOK'S TIP**

The proportions for the salsa verde can vary according to taste. As a rough guide, for 150 ml (1/4 pint) of olive oil, finely chop 50 g (2 oz) of herbs (basil, oregano, marjoram or parsley) and add to the oil. Mix in some lemon juice, a crushed or chopped clove of garlic, and season well. For speed, you can make this sauce in a blender or food processor.

# ORIENTAL SALAD

SERVES: 4 PREPARATION: 10 MINS COOKING: 10 MINS

## INGREDIENTS

For the omelette strips:
4 eggs
½ tsp soy sauce
vegetable oil for frying

For the dressing:
grated zest and juice of 1 lime
½ tsp salt
1 tsp brown sugar
2 tbsp sunflower oil

50 g (2 oz) peanuts
250 g (8 oz) sugar snap peas
1 yellow pepper, de-seeded and sliced
250 g (8 oz) mixed bean sprouts
2 tbsp chopped fresh coriander

## NUTRITION

*Each portion contains:*
*Energy: 290 calories*
*Fat: 21 g of which saturates 4 g*

1 For the omelette strips, beat the eggs with the soy sauce. Using a little oil, cook in a small frying pan to make two or three thin omelettes. Leave to cool, then roll each of them up and cut into narrow strips.

2 Mix the dressing ingredients together.

3 Preheat the oven to 200°C/400°F/gas 6. Roast the peanuts in the oven for 3–4 minutes, then chop coarsely. Set aside.

4 Blanch the sugar snap peas in boiling water for 1 minute, then drain and cool. Mix with the yellow pepper and bean sprouts. Pour over the dressing and mix well.

5 Garnish the salad with the omelette strips, coriander and peanuts just before serving.

### COOK'S TIP

This is a light salad packed with nutrients. Bean sprouts are a good source of vitamins, and the peanuts and omelette provide protein. Mung bean sprouts are widely available. They are sweet and tender, but watch out for ungerminated seeds which can be bullet-hard. Chick pea sprouts have a good crunch, but should be really fresh or they can be sour. Sweet-tasting alfalfa sprouts, whilst a great source of vitamins, are better as a garnish for salad as they have such a fine texture they can get easily lost when mixed with other ingredients.

# STUFFED TOMATOES WITH FETA AND ALMONDS

SERVES: 4 PREPARATION: 15 MINS COOKING: 25 MINS

INGREDIENTS

50 g (2 oz) flaked or chopped blanched almonds
75 g (3 oz) couscous
¼ tsp salt
200–250 ml (7–8 fl oz) boiling water
4 large tomatoes
125 g (4 oz) feta cheese, crumbled
2 sticks celery, finely diced
2 tbsp chopped fresh parsley
2 tbsp chopped fresh mint
1 tbsp olive oil
salt and pepper

NUTRITION

*Each portion contains:*

*Energy: 240 calories*

*Fat: 17 g of which saturates 5 g*

1 Preheat the oven to 200°C/400°F/gas 6. Roast the almonds in the oven for 4–5 minutes or until golden brown. Shake the pan once or twice during roasting so that the almonds brown evenly. Reduce the oven heat to 190°C/375°F/gas 5 ready to cook the stuffed tomatoes.

2 Soak the couscous in the salted boiling water for 5 minutes. Drain if necessary.

3 Cut a lid from each tomato and set aside. Scoop out the seeds and central flesh. Mix the couscous with the toasted almonds, crumbled feta, celery, parsley, mint and oil. Season well. Pile the filling into the tomato shells and top with the lids. Bake for 15–20 minutes. Serve immediately.

**COOK'S TIP**

Couscous mixed with feta and almonds makes a simple savoury filling for tomatoes. These can be served with a green salad or green vegetables.

# ROAST VEGETABLES WITH TOMATO SAUCE

SERVES: 4 PREPARATION: 15 MINS COOKING: 20–25 MINS

## INGREDIENTS

6 tbsp olive oil
salt and pepper
1 medium aubergine, de-seeded and cubed
175 g (6 oz) baby sweetcorn
4 courgettes, sliced
350 g (12 oz) plum tomatoes, halved
50 g (2 oz) pine kernels
1 clove garlic, peeled
1 tsp fresh thyme or marjoram

## NUTRITION

*Each portion contains:*

*Energy: 315 calories*

*Fat: 27 g of which saturates 3 g*

1 Preheat the oven to 200°C/400°F/gas 6. Season 4 tbsp of the olive oil, then toss with the vegetables so that the pieces are lightly coated with oil. Spread the aubergine, sweetcorn and courgettes on a large baking sheet, and the tomato halves on a separate baking sheet. Roast in the oven for 20–25 minutes, until soft and well-browned.

2 Roast the pine kernels on a baking sheet in the oven for 2–3 minutes or until just beginning to brown. Set aside.

3 Put all the roast tomatoes into a blender and add the remaining olive oil, the garlic and herbs. Blend until smooth. Season to taste.

4 Arrange the roast aubergine, sweetcorn and courgettes on a platter or individual plates and pour over some of the tomato sauce. Scatter the pine kernels on top. Serve immediately.

## COOK'S TIP

This simple dish can be made with a variety of vegetables in season. Peppers work well, as do baby artichokes or thick slices of field mushrooms. For a light supper serve the roast vegetables with good rustic bread and a mixed leafy green salad. For a more substantial meal accompany with rice or couscous. This tomato sauce is a useful quick topping for pasta as well as steamed green vegetables such as broccoli or fine green beans. If you make it in advance, reheat it gently; do not boil or you will lose some of the fresh flavour.

# CASHEW AND BEAN SPROUT STIR-FRY WITH THREE-COLOURED VEGETABLES

SERVES: 4 PREPARATION: 10 MINS COOKING: 10 MINS

## INGREDIENTS

1 tbsp sunflower oil
1 clove garlic, peeled and chopped
125–175 g (4–6 oz) cashew nut pieces
350 g (12 oz) bean sprouts
1 red pepper, de-seeded and thinly sliced
250 g (8 oz) baby sweetcorn, roughly chopped
250 g (8 oz) courgettes, cut in sticks
2 tbsp soy sauce
2 tbsp dry sherry
juice of ½ lemon
2 tsp sesame oil

## NUTRITION

*Each portion contains:*

*Energy: 340 calories*

*Fat: 22 g of which saturates 4 g*

1 Heat the sunflower oil in a wok or large frying pan and quickly stir-fry the garlic and cashew pieces until golden. Add all the vegetables and continue stir-frying until they are just tender but still crisp.

2 Mix together the soy sauce, sherry, lemon juice and sesame oil and pour this over the vegetables. Toss the mixture so that it is all well-flavoured, then serve immediately.

### COOK'S TIP

This recipe is quick, colourful and nutritious as well and lends itself to many variations. I like to include bean sprouts as they are moist and succulent. Other combinations that work well with the cashews are yellow pepper, mange tout and carrot; fine green beans, baby plum tomatoes and mushrooms; asparagus, red pepper and carrot; or sugar snap peas, mushrooms and baby sweetcorn.

*See full picture on page 41.*

# GREEN BEAN AND SWEETCORN SAUTÉ

SERVES: 4 PREPARATION: 10 MINS COOKING: 15 MINS

## INGREDIENTS

50 g (2 oz) hazelnuts
2 tbsp) olive oil
2 cloves garlic, peeled and sliced
250 g (8 oz) green beans, halved crosswise
250 g (8 oz) baby sweetcorn, halved crosswise
50 ml (2 fl oz) vegetable stock or water
salt and pepper

## NUTRITION

*Each portion contains:*
*Energy: 225 calories*
*Fat: 14 g of which saturates 1.5 g*

1 Preheat the oven to 190°C/375°F/gas 5. Roast the hazelnuts in the oven for 5–6 minutes. Leave to cool, then rub off the skins. Chop coarsely.

2 Heat the oil in a sauté pan or frying pan with a lid and cook the sliced garlic over a low heat until soft. Increase the heat and add the green beans and sweetcorn. Fry for 2–3 minutes, stirring to make sure the vegetables are coated with oil. Pour on the stock or water. Cover the pan, reduce the heat and cook for 5–6 minutes or until the vegetables are just tender.

3 Toss in the chopped hazelnuts and season well. Serve hot.

### COOK'S TIP

This is a light colourful dish that works well both as a quick supper or lunch served with rice or noodles. It also makes a good accompaniment to risotto and pastry dishes such as the Spinach and Feta Quiche (page 56).

*See full picture on page 40.*

# TEN-MINUTE STANDBY SUPPER

SERVES: 2 PREPARATION: 5 MINS COOKING: 5 MINS

INGREDIENTS

150 g (5 oz) couscous
salt and pepper
3 tbsp olive oil
1 red onion, peeled and chopped
1 red pepper, de-seeded and cut in thin slices
2 courgettes, sliced
75 g (3 oz) pine kernels
175 g (6 oz) cup mushrooms, sliced
1–2 tsp pesto sauce

NUTRITION

*Each portion contains:*

*Energy: 335 calories*

*Fat: 23 g of which saturates 2 g*

1 Put the couscous into a bowl, add a pinch of salt and cover with 200 ml (7 fl oz) boiling water. Leave to soak for 5 minutes while you prepare the stir-fry.

2 Heat 1 tbsp of the oil in a wok or large frying pan and stir-fry the red onion over a high heat. Add the red pepper, courgettes and pine kernels and stir-fry for about 3 minutes. Finally, add the mushrooms and stir-fry until quite soft. Stir in the pesto and season to taste.

3 Fluff up the couscous with a fork, adding the remaining olive oil. Pile on to plates and top with the stir-fry vegetables.

## COOK'S TIP

This is a nutritious meal which can be just about prepared and cooked in 10 minutes, and that includes getting the accompanying couscous ready. For 4 people just double the quantities, but note that it will take just a bit longer to make. You can, of course, vary the combination of vegetables. Ready-made pesto sauce is widely available, but varies enormously in terms of flavour. If you have a plentiful supply of basil in the summer, make your own. Grind some pine kernels with basil leaves and garlic, then add a good-quality olive oil. You can then add Parmesan cheese, sun-dried tomatoes or cashew nuts. The final consistency should be thick and fairly smooth. Whether home-made or shop-bought, pesto should be kept in the refrigerator once opened.

# SPINACH TAGLIATELLE WITH BUTTON MUSHROOMS AND HAZELNUTS

SERVES: 4 PREPARATION: 10 MINS COOKING: 10 MINS

## INGREDIENTS

50 g (2 oz) hazelnuts
4 tbsp olive oil
300 g (10 oz) button mushrooms, finely sliced
2 cloves garlic, peeled and crushed
salt and pepper
300–350 g (10–12 oz) spinach tagliatelle
10–25 g (½ –1 oz) butter
3–4 tbsp finely chopped fresh parsley
freshly grated Parmesan to serve

## NUTRITION

*Each portion contains:*
*Energy: 470 calories*
*Fat: 23 g of which saturates 4 g*

1 Preheat the oven to 200°C/400°F/gas 6. Roast the hazelnuts in the oven for 5–6 minutes. Rub off the skins and chop coarsely.

2 Heat the oil in a frying pan and fry the mushrooms with the garlic on a high heat until well browned. Season well. Add the hazelnuts and fry for a few more minutes.

3 Meanwhile, cook the pasta in a large pan of boiling salted water until just tender.

4 Drain the pasta and toss with the butter, then add the cooked mushroom mixture and parsley and toss well. Serve immediately with a separate bowl of grated Parmesan.

### COOK'S TIP

A simple sauté of succulent vegetables works very well with pasta and makes a change from lashings of sauce. I serve this with a tomato salad.

# WHOLEMEAL PASTA SHELLS WITH SUMMER VEGETABLES

SERVES: 4 PREPARATION: 10 MINS COOKING: 10 MINS

## INGREDIENTS

300–350 g (10–12 oz) wholemeal pasta shells
300 ml (½ pint) double cream
1 shallot, peeled and finely chopped
125 g (4 oz) green beans, sliced
125 g (4 oz) shelled fresh peas
125 g (4 oz) courgettes, sliced
1–2 tbsp finely chopped fresh mint
salt and pepper

## NUTRITION

*Each portion contains:*

*Energy: 620 calories*

*Fat: 38 g of which saturates 22 g*

1 Cook the pasta in a large pan of boiling salted water for 10 minutes or until just tender.

2 Meanwhile, heat the cream with the shallot in a large pan. Bring gently to the boil, then leave to simmer gently while you prepare the vegetables. Steam or microwave the vegetables until just tender. Drain well. Mix the vegetables into the cream sauce.

3 Drain the pasta and quickly mix into the cream sauce. Add the fresh mint. Season well. Serve immediately.

### COOK'S TIP

For a dairy-free version of this recipe do not use double cream. Instead toss the cooked pasta with well-seasoned olive or walnut oil and then toss in the vegetables. Top with some toasted nuts. Alternatively, ring the changes by using broccoli or cauliflower florets or broad beans.

# PASTA WITH SAUTÉ SPINACH AND SHALLOTS

SERVES: 4 PREPARATION: 5 MINS COOKING: 15 MINS

INGREDIENTS

50 g (2 oz) butter
50 g (2 oz) breadcrumbs
300–350 g (10–12 oz) wholemeal pasta spirals
2 shallots, peeled and finely chopped
1–2 tsp Dijon mustard
450 g (1 lb) spinach, rinsed and dried

NUTRITION

*Each portion contains:*
*Energy: 420 calories*
*Fat: 13 g of which saturates 7 g*

*See full picture on page 50.*

1 Melt half of the butter in a frying pan and fry the breadcrumbs until crisp. Set aside.

2 Cook the pasta spirals in a large pan of boiling salted water until just tender.

3 Meanwhile, melt the remaining butter in a large saucepan and cook the shallots for 3 minutes or until just soft. Add the mustard and mix in well. Tear or snip the spinach leaves into small pieces and drop them into the pan. Keep the heat high and continue cooking until the spinach is just wilted.

4 Drain the pasta and toss it with the spinach and shallot mixture, then quickly mix in the breadcrumbs and serve immediately.

**COOK'S TIP**

Despite this dish having four stages, it can be prepared, cooked and on the table in less than 20 minutes. I like the colour combination of spinach with wholemeal pasta, but a plain or egg pasta would work as well. This dish really needs nothing with it, although you could serve a tomato salad or some sauté mushrooms if you have time. Freshly grated Parmesan is also a nice addition.

# POLENTA WITH ROAST CHILLI SAUCE

SERVES: 4 PREPARATION: 15 MINS COOKING: 1½ HOURS

INGREDIENTS

200 g (7 oz) coarse polenta
1 tsp salt
50 g (2 oz) margarine or butter
125 g (4 oz) mature Cheddar cheese, grated

For the sauce:
1 fresh green chilli
2 tbsp sunflower oil
1 onion, peeled and finely chopped
2 cloves garlic, peeled and crushed
2 peppers (red or green), de-seeded and diced
1 tsp dried oregano
½ tsp ground cinnamon
400 g (14 oz) tin chopped tomatoes
salt and pepper

NUTRITION

*Each portion contains:*
*Energy: 500 calories*
*Fat: 28 g of which saturates 14 g*

1 To cook the polenta, bring up to a litre (1¾ pints) of water and the salt to the boil in a large saucepan and slowly pour in the polenta, stirring constantly. Leave to simmer until cooked (see Cook's Tip).

2 Stir in the margarine or butter and pour the mixture into a greased dish. Leave to cool, then cut into small squares.

3 For the sauce, preheat the oven to 200°C/400°F/gas 6. Roast the chilli in the oven for 10 minutes. Leave to cool, then peel and remove the seeds. Chop the flesh finely. Leave the oven on for cooking the polenta.

4 Heat the oil in a saucepan and gently fry the onion and garlic until soft. Add the chilli and diced peppers and cook for 5–10 minutes over a gentle heat. Stir in the oregano, cinnamon and tomatoes. Bring to the boil, then simmer for 20 minutes. Season to taste.

5 Put the squares of polenta in a shallow ovenproof dish. Spoon over the sauce, then cover with grated cheese. Bake in the preheated oven for 20–25 minutes or until the cheese has melted and browned and the polenta is heated through. Serve immediately.

COOK'S TIP

Polenta may vary from one brand to another, so it is important to double-check the instructions on the packet, as they may differ from those given above.

*See full picture on page 51.*

# MICROWAVE RISOTTO WITH CARROT AND COURGETTE

SERVES: 4 PREPARATION: 10 MINS COOKING: 17 MINS

## INGREDIENTS

2 tbsp olive oil
1 onion, finely chopped
250 g (8 oz) arborio rice
2 sticks celery, finely diced
1 litre (1¾ pints) vegetable stock
2 carrots, peeled and grated
1 courgette, grated
salt and pepper
25–50 g (1–2 oz) butter
2 tbsp freshly grated Parmesan

## NUTRITION

*Each portion contains:*

*Energy: 380 calories*

*Fat: 14 g of which saturates 6 g*

1 In a large dish suitable for a microwave, mix the oil and onion. Cook for 1 minute. Stir in the rice and celery and cook for 1 more minute. Stir well again, then pour over the vegetable stock. Cook for 5 minutes. Stir well again, then add the grated carrots and courgette.

2 Cook for a further 4 minutes, and check on the liquid content, adding a little more if necessary. Then cook for a further 4 minutes. Stir again and check if the rice is cooked. If not, cook for a further 2 minutes, adding more liquid if necessary.

3 Season well and add the butter and Parmesan cheese. Serve immediately with extra Parmesan cheese.

### COOK'S TIP

Cook this in a covered dish, on high (600W) throughout. I tried shock-horror tactics on an Italian friend when I told her how I found the microwave useful for making risotto. Far from passing out, she saw the value of creating a delicious creamy rice dish without being tied to the stove for well over half an hour. True, the end result does not have quite the authentic texture of a slowly-stirred risotto but it makes a very acceptable substitute. You could also add finely chopped leeks, mushrooms or fennel. Arborio rice is a special short-grain rice used for risottos. The grains swell during cooking and stick together. It is available in supermarkets.

# MUSHROOM AND ALMOND RICE WITH CHILLI

SERVES: 4 PREPARATION: 10 MINS COOKING: 40 MINS

## INGREDIENTS

1–2 large fresh mild green chillies
2 tbsp olive oil
1 onion, peeled and very finely chopped
2 cloves garlic, peeled and crushed
125 g (4 oz) button mushrooms, finely chopped
125 g (4 oz) long-grain brown rice
125 g (4 oz) wild rice
50 g (2 oz) blanched almonds, toasted and chopped
600 ml (1 pint) boiling vegetable stock or water
2–3 tbsp finely chopped fresh parsley, plus whole leaves to garnish
salt and pepper

## NUTRITION

*Each portion contains:*

*Energy: 370 calories*

*Fat: 14 g of which saturates 1 g*

1 Preheat the oven to 200°C/400°F/gas 6. Roast the chillies in the oven for 10 minutes. Leave to cool, then remove the skin and seeds and chop the flesh.

2 Heat the oil in a saucepan and gently fry the onion and garlic until very soft. Add the mushrooms and cook until softened, then add the chopped chilli, the brown and wild rice and the almonds. Stir well so the rice grains are coated with oil and cook for 2 minutes.

3 Pour over the boiling stock or water. Bring to the boil, then simmer for 25–30 minutes or until the rice is cooked and the liquid has been absorbed. Check on the liquid towards the end of cooking and add more if necessary.

4 Stir in the parsley and seasoning, garnish with whole parsley leaves and serve immediately.

### COOK'S TIP

The dark colours of this dish look warm and rich, and the roast chilli adds a fiery hint. This is delicious served with grilled courgettes or steamed green beans and a separate bowl of plain yoghurt.

# SPINACH AND FETA QUICHE

SERVES: 4 PREPARATION: 10 MINS, PLUS 30 MINS CHILLING

COOKING: 35 MINS

## INGREDIENTS

For the pastry:

125 g (4 oz) wholemeal flour
pinch of salt
2 tbsp sesame seeds
50 g (2 oz) solid vegetable fat and/or butter, well chilled
1 tbsp sunflower oil
2–3 tbsp cold water

For the filling:

2 tbsp sunflower oil
1 onion, peeled and chopped
350 g (12 oz) spinach, rinsed
4 eggs
150 ml (¼ pint) single cream
150 ml (¼ pint) milk
salt and pepper
150 g (5 oz) feta cheese, crumbled
2 tbsp sesame seeds

## NUTRITION

*Each portion contains:*

*Energy: 660 calories*

*Fat: 51 g of which saturates 21 g*

1 Make the pastry by mixing the flour, salt and sesame seeds. Rub in the fat, then add the oil and enough water to bind to a dough. Wrap in cling film and chill for 30 minutes.

2 Preheat the oven to 200°C/400°F/gas 6. Roll out the dough and line a 20 cm (8 in) flan ring or tin. Bake in the oven for 5 minutes. Leave the oven on while you make the filling.

3 For the filling, heat the oil in a large pan and gently fry the onion until soft. Add the spinach and stir-fry over a high heat until it has wilted and the juices have boiled away. Leave to cool.

4 Whisk the eggs with the cream and milk and season well. Spread the spinach mixture in the pastry case. Sprinkle over the crumbled feta, then pour on the egg mixture. Scatter the sesame seeds over the top. Return to the oven and bake for 25 minutes. Serve warm.

### COOK'S TIP

Here the robust flavours of spinach and feta complement the wholemeal pastry base. I prefer quiche such as this served warm, but cold it could be part of a picnic spread. Serve this with colourful contrasting salads such as tomato or pepper and new potato.

# DEEP PAN PIZZA WITH ONION AND CAPER TOPPING

SERVES: 4 PREPARATION: 10 MINS, PLUS 1 HOUR RISING

COOKING: 35 MINS

INGREDIENTS

For the dough:

250 g (8 oz) strong white bread flour

1 tsp salt

1 packet easy blend dried yeast

4 tbsp milk

2 medium eggs, beaten

2 tbsp olive oil

For the onion topping:

3 tbsp olive oil

2–3 medium onions, peeled and cut into thin rings

salt and pepper

2 tbsp capers

NUTRITION

*Each portion contains:*

*Energy: 390 calories*

*Fat: 16 g of which saturates 3 g*

1 To make the dough, mix the flour, salt and yeast together in a large bowl. Warm the milk slightly, then add it to the bowl with the beaten eggs and olive oil. Work into a dough and knead well, until firm and elastic. The dough should have a soft, slack consistency; if it is too sticky, just knead in a little more flour.

2 Put the dough in a clean bowl and cover with cling film or a damp cloth. Leave in a warm place until well risen. This takes about an hour.

3 Knead the dough again. Lightly brush a 23 cm (9 in) tin or deep flan dish with oil. Put the dough in the tin and press it out to line evenly. Leave to rise for about 10 minutes.

4 Preheat the oven to 200°C/400°F/gas 6. To make the topping, heat 2 tbsp of the oil in a frying pan and gently cook the onions for about 10 minutes or until very soft and translucent. Season to taste.

5 Brush the pizza base with a little of the remaining oil. Spread the onion mixture over the base, then scatter on the capers. Drizzle the rest of the oil on top.

6 Bake the pizza for 15 minutes, then reduce the heat to 190°C/375°F/gas 5 and bake for a further 10 minutes. Serve hot, cut into wedges.

*See full picture on page 60.*

# WHOLEMEAL PIZZAS WITH TOMATO TOPPING

SERVES: 4 PREPARATION: 20 MINS, PLUS 1 HOUR RISING

COOKING: 12-15 MINS

## INGREDIENTS

For the dough:

350 g (12 oz) half strong wholemeal and half strong white bread flour
1 tsp salt
1 packet easy blend dried yeast
1 tbsp olive oil
200 ml (7 fl oz) warm water

For the tomato topping:

1–2 tbsp olive oil
1 onion, peeled and finely chopped
1 clove garlic, peeled and crushed
400 g (14 oz) tin chopped tomatoes
1 tsp dried oregano
salt and pepper
fresh basil leaves, to garnish (optional)

## NUTRITION

*Each portion contains:*

*Energy: 337 calories*

*Fat: 6 g of which saturates 1 g*

1 To make the dough, mix together the flours, salt and yeast in a large bowl. Add the olive oil and warm water and mix to a dough. Knead well until firm and elastic. Put into a clean bowl, cover with cling film and leave to rise in a warm place (this can take up to an hour).

2 Meanwhile, make the tomato topping. Heat the oil and gently fry the onion and garlic until soft. Add the chopped tomatoes and oregano and stir well. Bring to the boil, then simmer over a moderate heat, stirring frequently, until some of the liquid has evaporated and you are left with a rich pulp. Season to taste.

3 Knead the dough again, then roll out into a large square or rectangle. Place the pizza base on an oiled baking sheet. Spoon the tomato topping over the base and spread out evenly. Leave to rise again for 10-15 minutes.

4 Preheat the oven to 210°C/425°F/ gas 7. Bake in the oven for 12–15 minutes. Cut the pizza into squares and eat hot or at room temperature. If you wish, garnish with fresh basil leaves.

*See full picture on page 61.*

# WINTER VEGETABLE HOTPOT WITH HERBS

SERVES: 4 PREPARATION: 15 MINS COOKING: 1 HOUR

## INGREDIENTS

2 tbsp sunflower oil
1 onion, peeled and finely chopped
2 leeks, chopped
4 sticks celery, diced
4 medium-sized carrots, peeled and chopped
2 medium-sized parsnips, peeled and chopped
250 g (8 oz) swede, peeled and chopped
25 g (1 oz) red lentils or yellow split peas
1 tsp chopped fresh rosemary
1 tbsp finely chopped fresh thyme
3 tbsp finely chopped fresh parsley
1 bay leaf
300 ml (½ pint) vegetable stock
500 ml (16 fl oz) passata
salt and pepper

## NUTRITION

*Each portion contains:*

*Energy: 190 calories*

*Fat: 7 g of which saturates 1 g*

1 Heat the oil in a large pan and gently fry the onion until it is soft but not coloured. Add the leeks, celery, carrots, parsnips and swede. 'Sweat' the vegetables for 10 minutes by cooking them very gently over a low heat with a lid on and stirring occasionally.

2 Add the lentils, herbs and stock and stir to mix. Bring to the boil, cover and simmer for 45–50 minutes or until all the vegetables are tender. Season to taste and serve hot.

## COOK'S TIP

This simple vegetable casserole makes a good warming supper dish in the autumn and winter months. I like to cut the vegetables into quite large chunks so that they keep their character once cooked. This recipe also uses passata, which is a thick tomato sauce sold in most supermarkets, usually in jars. Serve this with baked or mashed potatoes.

# THREE-BEAN CHILLI

SERVES: 4 PREPARATION: 15 MINS COOKING: 1¼ HOURS

INGREDIENTS

3 tbsp olive oil
2 onions, peeled and roughly chopped
2 cloves garlic, peeled and crushed
1–2 fresh green chillies, de-seeded and chopped
1 tsp cumin seeds
5 cm (2 in) stick cinnamon
2 sticks celery, sliced
3 medium carrots, peeled and chopped
1 red pepper, de-seeded and chopped
400 g (14 oz) tin red kidney beans, drained and rinsed
400 g (14 oz) tin black eye or pinto beans, drained and rinsed
50 g (2 oz) green lentils,
500 ml (16 fl oz) passata
300 ml (½ pint) vegetable stock
salt and pepper

NUTRITION

*Each portion contains:*

*Energy: 370 calories*

*Fat: 10 g of which saturates 1.5 g*

1 Heat the oil in a large pan and gently fry the onions and garlic until soft but not coloured. Add the chillies, cumin seeds and cinnamon stick and fry for 2 minutes, stirring. Add the celery, carrots and red pepper and cook for 10 minutes, stirring occasionally.

2 Add the beans and lentils and mix in well. Pour on the passata and stock. Bring to the boil, then cover and simmer for 50–60 minutes. Remove the cinnamon stick, season well and serve hot.

**COOK'S TIP**

Of all the vegetarian casseroles, chilli is one of the most popular. The most successful chillis have plenty of colour and a range of textures, which is easily achieved by using different types of beans and a handful of lentils. Passata is a thick tomato sauce sold in most supermarkets, usually in jars. Serve this chilli with baked potatoes, rice or Corn Bread (page 15), plus a green vegetable or simple salad if you like.

# PUY LENTILS AND MUSHROOMS WITH RED WINE

SERVES: 4 PREPARATION: 10 MINS COOKING: 55 MINS

## INGREDIENTS

2 tbsp olive oil
1 onion, peeled and chopped
2 cloves garlic, peeled and crushed
250 g (8 oz) chestnut mushrooms, quartered
175 g (6 oz) Puy lentils
250 g (8 oz) carrots, peeled and diced
125 ml (4 fl oz) red wine
2 tsp soy sauce
4 tbsp passata
1 bay leaf
1 tsp dried thyme
2 tbsp finely chopped fresh parsley
salt and pepper

## NUTRITION

*Each portion contains:*

*Energy: 240 calories*

*Fat: 7 g of which saturates 1 g*

1 Heat the oil in a large pan and fry the onion and garlic until soft.

2 Add the mushrooms and cook for 10 minutes or until quite soft.

3 Add the lentils and carrots with the wine, soy sauce, water and passata. Stir in the herbs. Bring to the boil, then cover and cook for 40–45 minutes or until the lentils are just tender. Add more liquid if necessary. Remove the bay leaf, and season to taste. Serve hot.

### COOK'S TIP

This is a richly coloured casserole with distinctive, complex flavours. Passata is a thick tomato sauce sold by most supermarkets, usually in jars. Puy lentils are very tiny lentils of a deep green colour, which cook quickly. Serve this dish with baked potatoes and glazed shallots, steamed carrots or a green vegetable such as broccoli.

# SPICED TOFU AND VEGETABLE TAGINE

SERVES: 4 PREPARATION: 15 MINS COOKING: 50–60 MINS

## INGREDIENTS

1 tbsp sunflower oil
1 onion, peeled and finely chopped
3 cloves garlic, peeled and crushed
2.5 cm (1 in) piece of root ginger, peeled and grated
1 tsp ground cumin
1 tsp ground coriander
½ tsp ground cinnamon
2 bay leaves
2 red peppers, de-seeded and diced
350 g (12 oz) green beans, sliced
1 packet regular tofu, cut into bite-sized pieces
400 g (14 oz) tin chopped tomatoes
300 ml (½ pint) vegetable stock
2 tbsp tomato purée
salt and pepper
2–3 tbsp chopped fresh coriander to garnish

## NUTRITION

*Each portion contains:*

*Energy: 140 calories*

*Fat: 5 g of which saturates 0.7 g*

1 Heat the oil in a large pan and fry the onion, garlic and ginger until softened. Stir in the spices and bay leaves and fry for a few minutes.

2 Add the red peppers and green beans and cook very gently until they start to soften. Add the tofu to the vegetables, then add the tomatoes, vegetable stock and tomato purée and stir well. Bring to the boil. Simmer gently for 50–60 minutes. Season well. Remove the bay leaves, sprinkle with the chopped coriander and serve hot.

### COOK'S TIP

Casseroles such as this North African tagine work really well with an ingredient such as tofu, which can be bland unless cooked with a multitude of spices. In this dish the spices are aromatic rather than hot, and colour comes from the green beans and red pepper. If possible, cook this dish a day ahead so the flavours have time to develop – refrigerate when it has cooled, then re-heat gently. Serve with couscous, bulgar wheat or rice.

# BABY SPINACH WITH GINGER AND GARLIC

SERVES: 4 PREPARATION: 5 MINS COOKING: 10 MINS

## INGREDIENTS

2 tbsp olive oil
1 onion, peeled and finely chopped
1 clove garlic, peeled and crushed
2 cm (½ in) piece of root ginger, freshly grated
½ tsp turmeric
250 g (8 oz) baby spinach, rinsed
4 tomatoes, peeled and chopped
1 tbsp tomato purée
salt and pepper

## NUTRITION

*Each portion contains:*
*Energy: 100 calories*
*Fat: 6 g of which saturates 1 g*

1 Heat the olive oil in a large pan and gently fry the onion and garlic for 3–4 minutes or until just soft. Add the ginger and turmeric and cook, stirring, for 2–3 minutes.

2 Pat the spinach dry, add to the pan and cook until the leaves have wilted. Mix in the chopped tomatoes and tomato purée and heat through. Season to taste and serve immediately.

### COOK'S TIP

This is a delicious, moist side dish. Serve it hot with couscous or cold with Olive and Pepper Strudels (page 23). The best way to peel tomatoes is to dip them briefly in a bowl of almost boiling water, remove with a slotted spoon and the skins will peel off easily.

# SHREDDED LEEKS WITH WINE AND CRÈME FRAÎCHE

SERVES: 4 PREPARATION: 5 MINS COOKING: 5 MINS

## INGREDIENTS

50 g (2 oz) butter
350 g (12 oz) leeks, shredded lengthways
6 tbsp white wine
4–6 tbsp crème fraîche
1 tsp whole grain mustard
salt and pepper

## NUTRITION

*Each portion contains:*

*Energy: 180 calories*

*Fat: 17 g of which saturates 7 g*

1 Melt the butter in a large frying pan and gently sauté the leeks until they are soft.

2 Pour on the wine and cook until the liquid has almost all evaporated. Remove the pan from the heat and quickly stir in the crème fraîche and mustard. Season to taste. Serve immediately.

### COOK'S TIP

These buttery leeks are good served with pastry dishes, such as the Spinach and Feta Quiche on page 56. The addition of wine turns them from an everyday vegetable into something special.

# RATATOUILLE WITH LEMON AND YOGHURT

SERVES: 4 PREPARATION: 10 MINS COOKING: 35 MINS

## INGREDIENTS

3–4 tbsp olive oil
1 aubergine, cubed
1 onion, peeled and finely chopped
1 clove garlic, peeled and crushed
1 red or green pepper, de-seeded and chopped
4 courgettes, chopped
250 g (8 oz) mushrooms, halved or quartered
1 tsp dried thyme or marjoram
150 ml (¼ pint) passata
salt and pepper
2 eggs, beaten
300 ml (½ pint) plain yoghurt
1–2 tbsp lemon juice

## NUTRITION

*Each portion contains:*
*Energy: 223 calories*
*Fat: 13 g of which saturates 3 g*

1 Heat 2 tbsp of the olive oil in a large pan and quickly fry the cubes of aubergine; remove from the pan. Heat the remaining oil in the pan and cook the onion and garlic for 3–4 minutes or until just starting to soften.

2 Add the pepper, courgettes and mushrooms and cook gently for about 10 minutes. Return the cooked aubergine cubes to the pan and stir in the herbs and passata. Season well. Cook for 3–4 minutes, then spoon the mixture into a shallow ovenproof dish.

3 Preheat the oven to 180°C/350°F/gas 4. Mix together the eggs, yoghurt and lemon juice and pour evenly over the vegetables. Bake in the oven for 20 minutes. Serve hot.

### COOK'S TIP

This is a lovely way to make a bit more of a simple vegetable mixture. It works well with the classic ingredients for ratatouille as well as other vegetables, such as red onion, celery or green beans. Passata is a thick tomato sauce sold by most supermarkets, usually in jars. Serve this dish with a light grain dish such as a rice pilaff or a baked potato or as an accompaniment to a filo pastry pie.

# SWEET
## treats

# AMERICAN PANCAKES WITH APPLE AND CINNAMON

SERVES: 4 PREPARATION: 10 MINS COOKING: 5 MINS

INGREDIENTS

125–175 ml (4–6 fl oz) milk
25 g (1 oz) butter, melted
1 egg
150 g (5 oz) plain flour
2 tsp baking powder
2 tbsp caster sugar
½ tsp salt
1 eating apple, cut into small slivers
1 tsp ground cinnamon

NUTRITION

*Each portion contains:*

*Energy: 258 calories*

*Fat: 8 g of which saturates 5 g*

1 Beat the milk with the butter and egg. In a separate bowl, combine the flour, baking powder, sugar and salt. Pour over the milk mixture and whisk until smooth. Don't over-whisk the batter or the pancakes won't rise so well. Stir in the apple and cinnamon.

2 Heat a small non-stick frying pan or griddle over a moderate heat. Pour in some batter and tilt the pan to make a pancake about 10 cm (4 in) across and 1 cm (½ in) thick. Cook for a few minutes or until well risen and full of holes. Flip over and cook on the other side. Tip the pancake out of the pan and keep hot while you make the remaining pancakes. Serve hot.

**COOK'S TIP**

American pancakes make a delicious breakfast with a difference. They are sweet and light, smaller and thicker than British pancakes or crêpes. If you wish, you can place a mould inside the frying pan to help the pancake hold its shape. If possible, serve with a good-quality maple syrup.

# ICED CARROT CAKE

SERVES: 8–10 PREPARATION: 10 MINS

COOKING: 1 HOUR–1 HOUR 20 MINS

## INGREDIENTS

For the cake:

250 g (8 oz) wholemeal flour
1 tbsp ground cinnamon
1 tsp grated nutmeg
2 tsp baking powder
125 g (4 oz) butter or margarine
125 g (4 oz) light muscovado sugar
125 g (4 oz) maple syrup
250 g (8 oz) carrots, peeled and finely grated
50 g (2 oz) walnuts, chopped
50 g (2 oz) sultanas

For the topping:

zest of 1 orange, taken in fine shreds
175 g (6 oz) cream cheese
50 g (2 oz) icing sugar, sifted

## NUTRITION

*Each portion contains:*

*Energy: 415–515 calories*

*Fat: 22–28 g of which saturates 12–15 g*

1 Preheat the oven to 160°C/325°F/gas 3. To make the cake, mix together the flour, spices and baking powder in a large bowl. Melt the butter or margarine with the sugar and maple syrup, then stir into the flour. Add the grated carrots, walnuts and sultanas. Mix everything thoroughly.

2 Spoon the mixture into a well-greased 450 g (1 lb) loaf tin. Bake in the oven for between 1 hour and 1 hour 20 minutes or until firm to the touch and a skewer inserted into the centre comes out clean. Leave the cake to cool in the tin for 10 minutes, then turn out onto a cooling rack.

3 To make the topping, blanch the orange zest in boiling water for 5 minutes; drain. Beat the cream cheese with the icing sugar until smooth. Mix in the orange zest. Spread thickly over the cake. Serve in thin slices.

### COOK'S TIP

Sweet and moist, this is a very easy cake to make and even easier to eat! You can serve it at tea time or as an alternative to pudding. If you want something plainer or dairy-free, skip the icing.

# BREAKFAST MUFFINS

SERVES: 4 PREPARATION: 10 MINS COOKING: 20 MINS

## INGREDIENTS

250 g (8 oz) wholemeal flour
125 g (4 oz) soft brown sugar
2 tsp baking powder
¼ tsp salt
1 tsp mixed spice
1 egg, beaten
250 ml (8 fl oz) milk
50 g (2 oz) melted butter, or 50 ml (2 fl oz) sunflower oil

## NUTRITION

*Each portion contains:*

*Energy: 185 calories*

*Fat: 8 g of which saturates 3 g*

1 Preheat the oven to 200°C/400°F/gas 6. Mix together the flour, sugar, baking powder, salt and spice. In a jug, mix together the egg, milk and melted butter or oil. Add the wet ingredients to the dry ones and mix until combined. Spoon the mixture into 12 muffin or deep bun tins. Bake in the oven for 20 minutes.

2 Variations: Once you have become familiar with the basic mixture, you can try many variations. Add ingredients such as bran or oats to replace a little of the flour. Add 125 g (4 oz) chopped nuts or dried fruits such as dates or sultanas, or a similar quantity of fresh fruits such as blueberries.

### COOK'S TIP

These are very easy, plain muffins, quick to make and bake in 20 minutes. They are ideal served at a special breakfast or brunch, as well as being useful for lunch box snacks.

# APRICOT AND PECAN CRUMBLE

SERVES: 4–6 PREPARATION: 15 MINS, PLUS 3–4 HOURS SOAKING

COOKING: 40 MINS

## INGREDIENTS

For the filling:

175 g (6 oz) dried apricots, chopped
2 tbsp marmalade
grated zest and juice of 1 orange

For the crumble topping:

75 g (3 oz) sunflower margarine
75 g (3 oz) wholemeal flour
75 g (3 oz) rolled oats
50 g (2 oz) soft brown sugar
50 g (2 oz) pecan nuts

## NUTRITION

*Each portion contains:*

*Energy: 335–500 calories*

*Fat: 17–26 g of which saturates 3–5 g*

1 Put the apricots in a saucepan, pour over enough hot water to cover and leave to soak for 3–4 hours.

2 Bring the apricots to the boil in the soaking water, then cover and cook for 20 minutes. The apricots should be fairly soft. Mix in the marmalade and orange zest and juice. Put the mixture into a greased ovenproof dish. Add a little more water if necessary so the fruit is moistened.

3 Preheat the oven to 180°C/350°F/gas 4. To make the crumble topping, rub the margarine into the flour, then add the oats and sugar. Reserve 8 pecan nut halves and coarsely chop the rest. Add these to the mixture. Sprinkle the crumble topping on the fruit. Arrange the whole pecan nuts on top.

4 Bake the crumble in the oven for 20–25 minutes. Serve hot.

### COOK'S TIP

Most dried fruit makes an excellent base for a crumble, being naturally sweet and highly nutritious. As the flavour is quite concentrated, try mixing dried fruit with fresh fruit or, as in this recipe, with a few tablespoons of marmalade which give a marvellous tang.

# PEAR BRÛLÉE

SERVES: 4–6 PREPARATION: 15 MINS COOKING: 40 MINS

INGREDIENTS

For the filling:
700 g (1½ lb) ripe pears
juice of ½ lemon
2–3 tbsp sugar

For the custard:
4 egg yolks
25 g (1 oz) caster sugar
½ tsp vanilla essence
300 ml (½ pint) cream
250 g (8 oz) fromage frais

For the caramel:
125 g (4 oz) golden granulated sugar
4 tbsp water

NUTRITION

*Each portion contains:*
*Energy: 350–530 calories*
*Fat: 16–24 g of which saturates 9–13 g*

1 Preheat the oven to 150°C/300°F/gas 2. Peel and core the pears and chop coarsely. Cook them very gently in a saucepan over a low heat with the lemon juice, covering the fruit with a butter paper. When soft, mash roughly with a fork, adding sugar to taste. Divide the mixture among 4–6 buttered ramekin dishes.

2 To make the custard, beat the egg yolks with the sugar and vanilla essence. Heat the cream until almost boiling, then stir into the egg yolk mixture. Add the fromage frais and mix well. Divide the custard among the ramekin dishes.

3 Place the dishes in a baking tray and pour boiling water round them to come up to the level of the custard. Bake in the oven for 30–35 minutes or until the custard has just set.

4 For the caramelised topping, dissolve the sugar in the water, then bring to the boil and boil vigorously until the mixture darkens. This takes about 5 minutes. Pour quickly over the custard and leave to set. Serve chilled.

**COOK'S TIP**

These are individual rich custards with a fruit base and caramelised topping. The fromage frais gives the mixture the taste and consistency of cheesecake, denser than traditional crème brûlée but equally delicious.

# PAVLOVA WITH WINTER FRUITS IN GINGER SYRUP

SERVES: 6 PREPARATION: 15 MINS COOKING: 2 HOURS

## INGREDIENTS

For the meringue:

3 egg whites
pinch of salt
¼ tsp cream of tartar
175 g (6 oz) golden caster sugar
1 tbsp cornflour
1½ tsp white wine vinegar

For the ginger syrup:

25 g (1 oz) granulated sugar
150 ml (¼ pint) water
2 pieces of stem ginger in syrup, sliced

For the topping:

2 ripe mangoes, peeled, stoned and chopped
125 g (4 oz) fresh dates, stoned and chopped
1 star fruit, sliced
300 ml (½ pint) double cream

1 Preheat the oven to 140°C/275°F/gas 1.To make the meringue, beat the egg whites with the salt and cream of tartar until soft. Add the sugar 1 tsp at a time, whisking in well. Then beat in the cornflour and vinegar. Pile the meringue onto a piece of baking parchment to make a 20 cm (8 in) circle. Make an indentation in the centre.

2 Bake in the oven for about 2 hours. It is quite hard to tell when the meringue is cooked. If you are unsure, leave it undisturbed in the cooling oven. Leave to cool completely.

3 For the ginger syrup, gently heat the sugar and water until the sugar has dissolved. Bring to the boil, then add the stem ginger and simmer for 2 minutes. Leave to cool.

4 Toss the fruit in a little of the ginger syrup. Whip the cream and spoon into the indentation in the meringue. Cover with the fruit. Leave for an hour or so in the fridge before serving.

## NUTRITION

*Each portion contains:*

*Energy: 430 calories*

*Fat: 34 g of which saturates 15 g*

### COOK'S TIP

The quantity of syrup made here is ample for the recipe. Keep the surplus and use it as a quick topping for ice cream or serve drizzled over pancakes.

# RICOTTA CHEESECAKE WITH CARAMELISED PLUMS

SERVES: 4–6 PREPARATION: 15 MINS, PLUS SETTING TIME

COOKING: 20 MINS

## INGREDIENTS

For the base:
75 g (3 oz) wholemeal flour
75 g (3 oz) rolled oats
50 g (2 oz) golden caster sugar
75 g (3 oz) butter

For the filling:
250 g (8 oz) ricotta
200 g (7 oz) strained plain Greek yoghurt
1–2 tbsp clear honey
½ tsp vanilla essence
grated zest of 1 lemon

For the topping:
3–4 ripe plums
5–10 g (¼–½ oz) butter, melted
few drops of lemon juice
2–3 tsp demerara sugar

## NUTRITION

*Each portion contains:*

*Energy: 333–500 calories*

*Fat: 19–28 g of which saturates 12–18 g*

1 Preheat the oven to 180°C/350°F/gas 4. For the base, combine the flour, oats and sugar in a large bowl. Melt the butter, then pour over the dry ingredients and mix well. Press into the base of a lined 20 cm (8 in) springform cake tin. Bake in the oven for 20 minutes. Leave to cool.

2 To make the filling, beat the ricotta with the yoghurt and honey until very smooth. Add the vanilla essence and lemon zest. Taste and adjust the sweetening, if necessary. Spoon the topping over the cooled base and chill for at least 24 hours to set.

3 To make the topping, slice the plums very finely and spread out in one layer on a baking sheet. Mix together the melted butter and lemon juice and brush or drizzle over the sliced fruit, then sprinkle with demerara sugar. Grill until the sugar melts and bubbles. Leave to cool. Arrange the fruit slices over the cheesecake before serving.

## INDEX